KAROLIEN VAN CAUWELAERT
& KARIN VAN OPSTAL

# Carpets & Rugs

Every home needs a soft spot

**Lannoo**

# Content

| | |
|---|---|
| 06 | Introduction |
| 10 | **Arty** |
| 31 | How to |
| 32 | **Tactiles** |
| 55 | How to |
| 56 | INTERVIEW Koen Vanmechelen |
| 60 | **Colour** |
| 81 | How to |
| 82 | **Outdoor** |
| 103 | How to |
| 104 | INTERVIEW Francq Colors |
| 108 | **Patterns** |
| 127 | How to |
| 128 | **Shapes and sizes** |
| 151 | How to |
| 152 | INTERVIEW Muller Van Severen |
| 156 | **Traditional & transitional** |
| 177 | How to |
| 178 | **Floral** |
| 201 | How to |
| 202 | INTERVIEW Bazaar Velvet |
| 206 | Credits |

'The soul of the apartment is the carpet. From it are deduced not only the hues but the forms of all objects incumbent.

A judge at common law may be an ordinary man; a good judge of a carpet must be a genius.'

Edgar Allan Poe
*Philosophy of Furniture* (1840)

Recently, we added a modern extension to our terraced house. In contrast to the thirties façade of the old house, it has a huge window overlooking the street. Behind the window is an office. When considering different possibilities for the floor coverings – tiles, wood, vinyl, laminate – it suddenly dawned on us. If we wanted the space to be both absolutely serene and at the same time snug and cosy, only one item could achieve that: a carpet. So we went for a soft beige carpet, and today, half a year later, we are still over the moon with it. When you enter our office, a soft quiet descends on you. The air is calm; the atmosphere is intimate. It is the perfect place to concentrate and work, and that is due to the calming effect of that simple expanse of carpet.

*What is it about carpets?* How is that they have been part of our interiors since the beginning of time, from the first bearskin on the cave floor to the precious Savonnerie carpets of Château de Versailles? The secret lies in their versatility. *Carpets cater to our senses*; they keep the cold out and are warm and soft to the touch. They caress our naked feet. *But carpets are storytellers, too.* They tell a story of materials, craftsmanship and creativity, possibly from a long-gone era. Last but not least, they tell a story about their owners: Do they like vibrant colours or neutral hues? Do they prefer flowers or abstract images? Shaggy and soft or trim and tight? Whatever their style or period, carpets will give an interior its proper stamp. They will determine the atmosphere and relevance of the room.

## Revival of the Rug

Despite all their beneficial qualities, carpets have been playing second fiddle to natural floor coverings like wood and stone in recent decades. Carpets struggled with a reputation of being stuffy and old-fashioned, and the market was determined by quiet collections with speckles or mixed shades of the same colour, without flowers or graphics. But that has changed over the last couple of years. Both contemporary and classic rugs are due a comeback and are being increasingly integrated into interior designs again. From being a neutral and unobtrusive background or even absent, they are now being pushed to the forefront again and sometimes even considered the foundation on which further interior decoration of the space will be based. Colour and movement have made their entrée again; designs are becoming bolder, and crazy shapes are making an appearance. Today, carpets and rugs proudly define the room they are in, instead of providing the background picture.

As a result, rug collections in showrooms and shops are brimming with new, more daring designs, and standard sizes are being joined by exclusive, bespoke pieces. High-end furniture brands show off their own collections designed by renowned designers, and entire magazines are even devoted to rugs and carpets. Where does this renewed attention to carpets come from? Belgian trend forecaster and colour specialist Hilde Francq (see interview p.104) believes that interior trends find their origin in sociological phenomena. The coronavirus crisis and the advance of digitisation are two reasons why the popularity of rugs is on the rise.

Because of the COVID-19 pandemic and the associated lockdowns, people were forced to stay at home and to work from home. They didn't go travelling and instead focused on how they could make their houses more comfortable and more fun to dwell in. Soft carpets are perfect for adding warmth, comfort and atmosphere, but they do more than that: they also improve acoustics and insulate against extreme temperatures.

The other phenomenon that plays a role is the increasing digitisation of our society. The more digital our world becomes, the more we will appreciate the tactility of our surroundings: large velvety-soft sofas, fat cushions, comfy throws and, of course, the soft touch of a carpet under your feet. This is something that computers and apps can never provide, and that's why we will see more and more high-pile carpets, even 'wilderness carpets', in the near future.

## Your Own Soft Spot

According to trend forecaster Hilde Francq, carpet trends for the near future include high-pile carpets, ecological carpets and allergy-free carpets. That said, showrooms around the world are noticing that all styles of rugs are enjoying something of a renaissance. The reason for this is that, no matter the style of a rug (be it traditional, classic or contemporary), when it is in proportion to the dimensions of the room within which it is placed, it will always be a great asset. The rest is a matter of taste.

This is why, in this book, we want to offer the reader a wild variety of carpets that have one thing in common: they are all pure eye candy and deserve to be in the centre of the room. That goes without saying for the 'Arty carpets' (p.10), which essentially upgrade your floor to the status of 'fifth wall', covered with art. It is a great way to add sophistication to your home, and the good news is there's so much choice. We also take the opportunity in this book to rehabilitate the floral carpet (p.178), which has been suffering from a very antiquated reputation indeed. This book also caters to people who prefer a classic carpet, be it a unique, old or traditional one, or what we call a 'transitional rug': a modern rug that combines features of traditional rugs with contemporary ones, which makes them timeless and sometimes quite trendy (p.156). Perhaps, though, you are looking to make a statement. Apart from arty carpets, you can also go for a blast of colour (p.60), a crazy shape (p.128) or an extremely tactile, shaggy example (p.32). Last but not least, we catch on with a trend that has been popular for some years: the outdoor rug (p.82). Since the patio has become a fully-fledged outdoor room, an extension of our interior, we have started decorating it accordingly. That means comfortable sofas and recliners, dining room ensembles and hyper-equipped outdoor kitchens, but also outdoor carpets that set the mood of a proper outdoor living room and provide extra comfort.

All the above means that, in this book, we will cater to all tastes, with photographs of interiors featuring breathtaking carpet designs, whose inspirations range from ethnic traditions to computerised techniques. As a result, you will see plenty of unexpected inspirations and surprising combinations. Imagine a classic, Turkish-style rug in a contemporary living space, injecting colour and warmth in an otherwise minimalist interior. That is the power of the carpet!

It is time to put that soft spot in our homes into the limelight again and make it the focus of our living spaces. Enjoy the ride!

# 'You can't just sweep me under the rug like I won't come back stronger and better.'

Demetrius
Andrade

# Arty

So you've decided to upgrade your floor to the status of 'fifth wall' and cover it with art? Enter the Arty rug: the perfect way to add a touch of sophistication to your home.

Most of the time, artists' designs have nothing to do with the real world. They serve only one purpose: to express the innermost feelings and emotions of the designer or artist who is creating them. Think Jackson Pollock pouring and dripping his paint or Mark Rothko creating his stunning colour planes. It is artworks like these that have been a huge inspiration for the world of interior design, including rugs and carpets. The last few years in particular have seen a huge surge in the production of abstract, Arty carpet designs, thanks to a rapid improvement in rug design technology. The latest technologies now enable designers to experiment with countless colours and crazy shapes. Their creations are all about flow, colour and movement and can create a wonderful dynamic in otherwise static spaces.

Where do designers find their inspiration? It could literally be anywhere: a favourite painting or painting technique, an unforgettable landscape they once visited, the view of the ocean from their bedroom window … but they also tell stories of personal experiences and feelings. As American carpet designer Sigal Sasson once put it in an interview: 'Every design in our collection has a story and I focus on designing each rug like it was a work of art to be viewed by the world. They convey adventurous contemporary artistic vibes, layered textures and unusual colour combinations, sometimes based on my personal experience and feelings.'

You may think that abstract design is too 'modern' or too 'cold' for you, but there is an abstract design for everyone. Do you feel like your home is missing character and is in need of a stylish addition? Go for a statement rug that will put your stamp on the place. Are your walls and furnishings a mixture of beiges and 'greiges', which makes your space feel like an arctic zone? Arty carpets to the rescue! You can warm the place up with a soothing design that combines creamy shades with a delicate touch of colour. Abstract designs will fit perfectly in any modern environment, but don't be put off if you happen to live in a period house. If you choose carefully, an Arty rug can be perfect to offset its more traditional features.

← Spanish designer Jaime Hayon designed the carpet *Silhouette* for Nanimarquina: a beautiful composition of delicately drawn imaginary characters that cheers up the otherwise sparingly appointed room.

↑ *Apparence* by Belgian designer Xavier Lust for Nodus creates an optical illusion. Seen from one side it is reminiscent of ancient rusticated floors, while from the other side it looks like a perforated surface.

Arty

Arty

Carpets & Rugs

→ This quite audacious interior is designed by Sepúlveda Arquitectos: a carpet from the Cápsulas del Tiempo collection of the Mexican brand Balmaceda Studio offsets a well-filled bookcase.

↘ Abstract shapes and subtle hues characterise Kelly Behun's *Eclipse* design for The Rug Company. The result: a calming, airy space, evoking the phases of the moon.

# How to

... be sure you are dealing with an
arty rug of good quality

Pay attention to the quality of materials (natural
or not), the colour tones (the more shades, the more
detailed the colour changes) and the design itself
(pixelated or meticulously executed). Have a look at
the texture, too – the surface of a handmade rug will
be slightly irregular.

... know which room is best
for an arty carpet

This is a very personal choice, but generally
speaking an arty carpet with a bold design will come
into its own when it is given ample space –
for example, in a hallway. Obscuring a design with
furniture will break the spell.

... know which interior style
the arty carpet fits best

There is no such thing as a fixed rule, as again
this is a matter of personal choice. That said, an arty
carpet can bring a wonderful splash of vivid colour
to minimalist houses and rooms furnished in muted,
classic colours like beige, grey and greige.

# Tactiles

In this chapter natural materials are to the fore. Each natural material has different tactile properties and therefore gives a different atmosphere to the room.

We wrote this book in 2021, when the COVID crisis contributed to an atmosphere of doom and gloom. Yet during the lockdowns there was also a positive note. Working from home became more and more important. Precisely because we have become more dependent on our interior, comfort and a touch of luxury are more important than ever before. In addition to richly upholstered materials, velvety carpets are the go-to of choice. Give someone the feeling of walking on clouds, and you score points immediately. In short, texture and tactility – how a material feels – have never been more important in the home.

In this chapter, of course, natural materials are to the fore. Each natural material has different tactile properties and therefore gives a different atmosphere to a room. Wool not only gives a feeling of cosiness and warmth, but also brings nature into the home. Silk is not just incredibly soft but also guarantees a luxurious shine. Leather is a warm, natural material that is generally smooth to the touch but can have rough edges. Think of cowhide or pigskin. Cotton rugs, on the other hand, are extremely child- and pet-friendly because they are so easy to maintain. And the once despised fitted carpet, so popular in the seventies and beyond, is back with a vengeance.

The tactile, natural rug has much more to offer than just warmth, comfort and atmosphere. A woolly rug also improves acoustics. Admittedly, pounding footsteps, loud music or bickering toddlers will not disappear into the ether completely, but shrill sounds are partially muffled or absorbed. A rug also provides insulation, with a high-pile rug retaining more heat than a low-pile one. Moreover, we have excellent news for those among us who suffer from allergy complaints due to house dust mites. There is absolutely no reason to keep a carpet out of your home. Precisely because carpets attract dust and pollen, all the dust is collected in one place instead of floating merrily around the house. It is just a matter of bringing out the vaccum cleaner in time. Furthermore, carpets made of natural fibres such as jute and sisal are thought to have a neutralising effect.

In short, tactility and texture provide welcome warmth in the home. Precisely because of the never-ending popularity of hardwood, concrete and cast floors, tactile carpets are more than ever here to stay.

↑ These very cuddly sheepskin collages are by Belgian designer Carine Boxy. Each handmade piece is unique and provides warmth, comfort and ambience in your home. In short, these rugs are the epitome of tactility.

Carpets & Rugs

← This soft, short-pile carpet from Brazilian brand Phenicia Concept and the wooden wall cabinet provide a warm counterweight in this brutalist home, where raw concrete with visible formwork grain sets the tone.

Tactiles

↑→ 'As pure as possible' turned out to be the motto when designing the *Pure* carpet made from handwoven wool and undyed biodegradable fibres. The woolly fringes provide a playful touch in this design by the Spanish duo Made Studio for GAN Rugs.

← The handwoven carpets from the Simla collection of British carpet house Jacaranda Carpets and Rugs are made of 100% Tencel. This eco-friendly material made of cellulose fibres is a valuable alternative to silk, thanks to its natural shine and velvety-soft touch and feel.

→ This carpet from the Art Deco collection by Revised brings the glamour of the 1920s and 1930s into your home. The Dutch designer Tjitske Storm has combined various materials and textures into a work of art that is as geometric as it is tactile.

→ How do you give a minimalist bathroom an instant upgrade? This carpet from the Nomad collection by the Antwerp carpet house Ashtari sets a good example. Its ethnic motifs, rough structures and glowing colours will let you turn down the thermostat a degree or two.

Carpets & Rugs

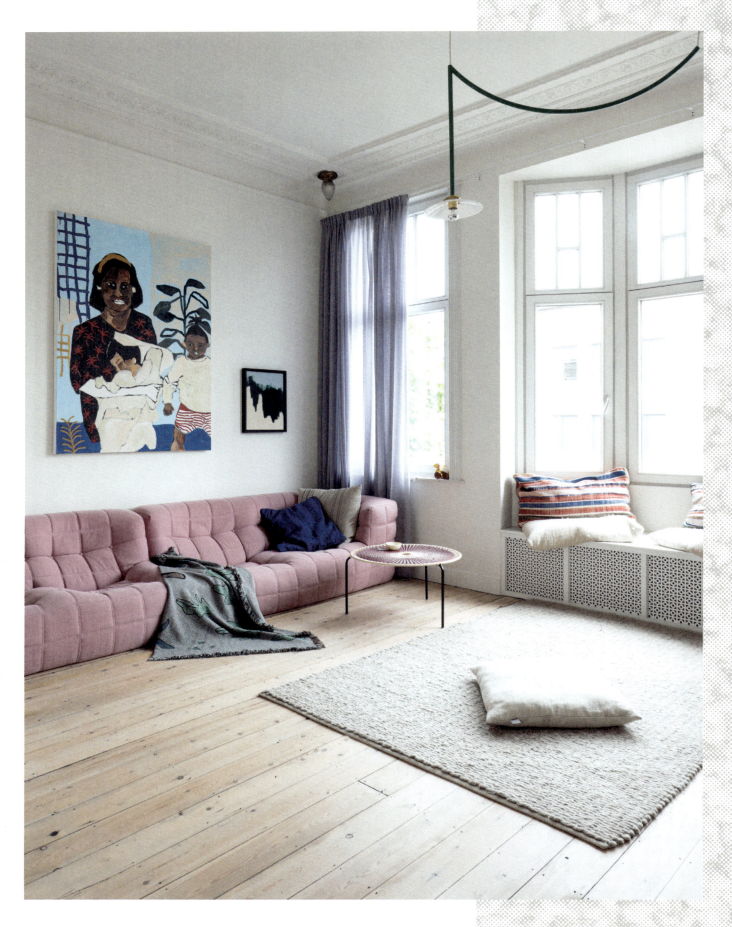

# How to

...    create an interior that is
both rough and warm
Mixed textures create an irresistible contrast.
Atmospheric earth tones and natural materials such
as wood and reed provide a warm counterbalance
to cool concrete with visible formwork grain, a steel
fireplace and rough, low-pile carpet.

...    create a soft, tactile interior
You can increase the tactile factor of a wool
rug, fluffy carpet or high-pile carpet by combining
it with a range of soft fabrics, such as velvet, fluffy
sheepskin, polar fleece or natural linen. Cushions,
plaids and warm earth tones also belong in a soft
living environment.

...    bring nature into your home
To create a natural, soothing atmosphere,
choose a sisal, jute or seagrass rug. It combines
perfectly with cognac-coloured leather, wooden
furniture, wicker chairs, fresh green houseplants and
other mood enhancers such as wool, rattan, bamboo
and linen.

# Koen Vanmechelen

The Belgian artist Koen Vanmechelen (born 1965) is an internationally acclaimed conceptual artist. His work explores the importance of global diversity, identity and community. He is best known for his Cosmopolitan Chicken Project (CCP) in which he cross-breeds domesticated chickens from different countries as a statement about global diversity. Over the years, the same examination of the ideas of diversity and identity can be found in his projects with pigs (LUCY), camelids and mushrooms (MECC) and cows (SOTWA) as well as in the Planetary Community Chicken Project (PCC). His aim is to encourage us to reach across borders, to come into contact with other cultures and hence to develop a mutual respect. Koen Vanmechelen's oeuvre comprises a unique mix of paintings, drawings, photographs, videos, installations, sculptures and textiles, and has been presented in numerous exhibitions on almost every continent, including the Venice Biennale. In addition, his scientific collaborations around his various projects have earned him several awards, including the Golden Nica Hybrid Art award in 2013.

WWW.LABIOMISTA.BE

## 'My work is not about chickens, it is about evolution.'

In 2019, he opened LABIOMISTA, an evolving artwork comprising 24 hectares of land including his studio and the Cosmopolitan Culture Park, on the site of the former Zoo of Zwartberg, in Genk, Belgium. Among his artworks are several carpets, of which the latest is a creation for the Dutch design brand Moooi Carpets.

**How did the rug you created for Moooi Carpets come about?**
'They contacted me to create a rug for their collections. Actually, this rug is a joint creation by myself and my chickens. I prepared a textile underlay with drawing, and put it on the floor in the chicken coop. Then I left it for them to decorate it in their own chicken way. Next, the rug was cleaned, but it kept its patina. Then it was my turn again to draw and paint.'

**What does the drawing refer to?**
'As in all my work, it is about crossbreeding. You see two heads, monstruous embryos searching for a way out to be born. You can see and feel the framework they are trying to escape. This work came about in specific circumstances. It was in the middle of the first wave of the COVID pandemic, and my wife had recently passed away. I was trapped in a double isolation, and threw myself on my painting, amid the chickens. That was how the work came about: me, locked up with my feelings and my chickens.'

**Generally speaking, a rug is a functional object. Is your creation art or design?**
'The carpet measures 380 x 460 centimetres, which is the exact surface of the chicken coop. The chickens determined the size of the carpet. If they hadn't, it would have been a question of design. Now it is simply part of my art. It will become part of an installation, together with the chickens and a video that was made during the creative process.'

**Why did you decide to work with Moooi Carpets?**
'Moooi Carpets has introduced a technology that generates extremely high-definition prints. As a result, they can create an endless mix of colours, illusions of depth and photo-realistic designs.'

**Your chickens tell a story that today is more pertinent than ever...**
'My work is not about chickens, it is about evolution, about breaching monoculture and about respecting nature. My research has shown that, after 20 generations of crossbreeding, all kinds of fortuitous mutations have occurred: my chickens have become more fertile and have better immunity. But still humanity has not understood the importance of reaching across borders. We are perfectly able to produce vaccines in order to contend with a pandemic, but we are not succeeding in developing a method for social recovery. We are not building factories around the world to combat the pandemic together. The issue should rise above politics, as it concerns humanity and how we want to progress, but sadly it hasn't. It is up to art to reveal society for what is: an artificial construct vis-à-vis a nature that is often ruthless, as recent developments have shown all too clearly.'

# Colour

This chapter is dedicated to all the colour addicts out there. To those who love a vibrant colour palette and give their interior the necessary boost. To those who know how to colour outside the box.

This includes the exceptionally talented among us, who, with their all-encompassing gaze, know how to jolly up any subdued, uncolourful interior. Let's face it: the world would be a dull place if only like-minded, like-coloured greige aficionados got their way.

In short, this is a chapter for the real daredevils among us. Because if we were to believe all those right-thinking interior decorators, we would all be living in sober interiors – soaked in muted sand and greige tones – brightened up as required with colourful accessories such as cushions and rugs, to create a different atmosphere. There is nothing wrong with that – but couldn't things be a bit spicier, sexier, bolder?

Choosing colour is not only a question of daring and courage. The impact of colour on your mood also goes under the radar. So let's let the colour psychologists have their say, too. For who are we to contradict the great Johann Wolfgang von Goethe when he states that 'experience shows that every colour gives a certain mood'? Yellow, for example, is said to radiate unbridled optimism, while green is the go-to for lovers of peace and nature. Blue is for accountants and analysts. And red is for passionate bon vivants and dominant characters. Check out those crimson high-heeled power shoes! In short, colour offers something for everyone.

But 'non-colours', such as white and black, also have a place in our colour bible. White is said to be the colour that can be combined with any other colour and that also best reflects light. In a nutshell, white is everyone's friend. Just like black. 'Because if you really don't know which colour to use, use black,' the great master Pablo Picasso once said.

There's just one more lesson to learn, and one that's an inspiration for the true romantics among us: delicate pastel shades such as blue, green and pink are more suitable for a children's room than a living room, and for a feminine interior rather than a masculine setting. But you probably already knew that.

↑ Does this rug remind you of something? Of course! Carpet *After Matisse* by designer Sonya Winner Studio is inspired by Henri Matisse's iconic paper cutouts. Handwoven, bright and cheerful, this stunning rug will be the eye-catching focus of your room. Or even of your whole house!

Colour

→ When Belgian designer Thibault Van Renne plays with lines and colours, the result is simple, timeless, yet unique. The *Artline* rug is hand-knotted, made of wool and silk, and has a unique oxidised finish to create a three-dimensional effect. Luxurious haute couture to dress up your floor.

↗ Time for some fun on the floor. The Squiggle rugs are a creation of a small Swedish-American design company Okey Studio. Squiggle rugs manage to be arty, funky, funny and cosy, all at the same time. Take a look at Okey Studio's Instagram account (@Okejstudio) to see all variations of Squiggles and the way they cheer up room after room.

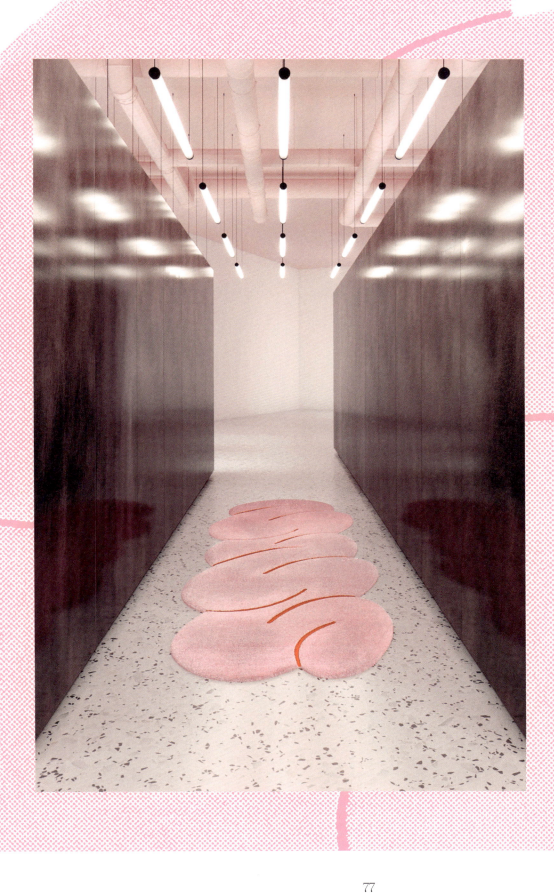

Colour

→ Graphic lines and bright daring colours characterise the oeuvre of Belgian designer and illustrator Klaartje Busselot. The *Pole Position* carpet from the FORM-ULA collection for design studio Kiiv is inspired by racetracks and whirling speed.

Carpets & Rugs

# How to

### ...   choose a bold, brightly coloured carpet for your living room

If you are looking for a bold statement rug, choose a neutral shade for the rest of your interior – for floors, walls and customised furniture, for example. But don't hesitate to let the bright colours of your rug return in accessories such as cushions, ceramics and other decorative items. Soft powder tones and bright fluorescent colours create a different atmosphere every time.

### ...   choose the right material

Colourful rugs give your interior an instant upgrade. But don't forget the heart-warming effect of warm materials and textures. Wood, textiles and natural stone provide a different texture and shade every time. They do not compete with a brightly coloured rug, but instead enhance the warming effect.

### ...   avoid overkill

Excess has a negative effect, not least when it comes to bright colours. Preferably, use colours that are inspired by nature. Fuchsia, for example, can be found in flowers, but there is no type of wood or stone that has this colour. It is best to use this bright, contrasting colour only for decorative objects and accessories.

# Outside

As George Michael knew, outside, in the sunshine, everything is better. Life in the open air makes you a happier person, as the outdoor sector has always understood. Around the turn of the millennium the patio rapidly began to emerge as a fully-fledged outdoor room, an extension of the interior.

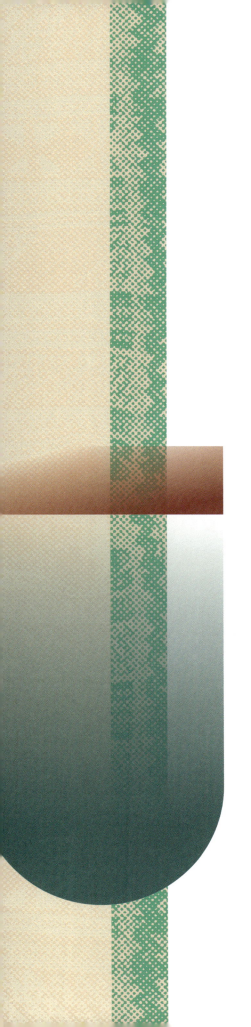

Inviting sofas and recliners, refined dining room ensembles that would not be out of place indoors, and hyper-equipped kitchens have successively made their appearance on the patio or terrace. At the same time, lighting, plants and other mood enhancers have been increasingly used. And last but not least, the outdoor carpet has made its appearance – because there is nothing better than a whisper-soft rug to transfer warmth from the inside to the outside world. An outdoor carpet helps not only to set the mood and provide extra comfort, but also to redefine the space.

An outdoor rug is usually a little more expensive to buy than its indoor counterpart. With an outdoor rug, there is so much more to consider – technology and weather resistance, for example. Nonetheless the ecological harms are limited. Outdoor rugs are increasingly made of sustainable polyester fibres and recycled materials such as PET – for example, from plastic waste fished out of the ocean.

Perhaps the most striking outdoor trend of the last decade has been the revolution in fabrics. Today's outdoor fabrics increasingly have the touch, feel and structure of indoor fabrics, whether it is a piece of furniture or a rug. Rugs have the added advantage that they can be edged with stylish piping or fringes. It is the details that make the difference.

Internationally renowned designers such as Paola Lenti, Jaime Hayon, Nani Marquina and Patricia Urquiola are also active in the outdoor furnishings sector. As a result, quite a few outdoor carpets are on the cusp of art and design. You will find them not only in a wide range of colours – from fruity raspberry through fresh aquamarine to subdued sage green – but also in subtle dégradé effects or in an artistic colour gradient where two colours slowly but fluently merge into one. In terms of motifs and patterns, too, the outdoor carpet is not inferior to its indoor sister. We have seen blossoming flower patterns (interesting if your garden is not in bloom during the winter), nostalgic lace, classic Scottish tartans, faceted diamonds, playful tile and checkerboard patterns and even a real miniature golf course! You name it, you'll find it.

← The handmade, flat-woven *Shade* rug by Turkish designer Begüm Cana Özgür for Spanish carpet brand Nanimarquina shows off an artful colour gradient where soft tones flow smoothly into one another. An inspired ode to nature.

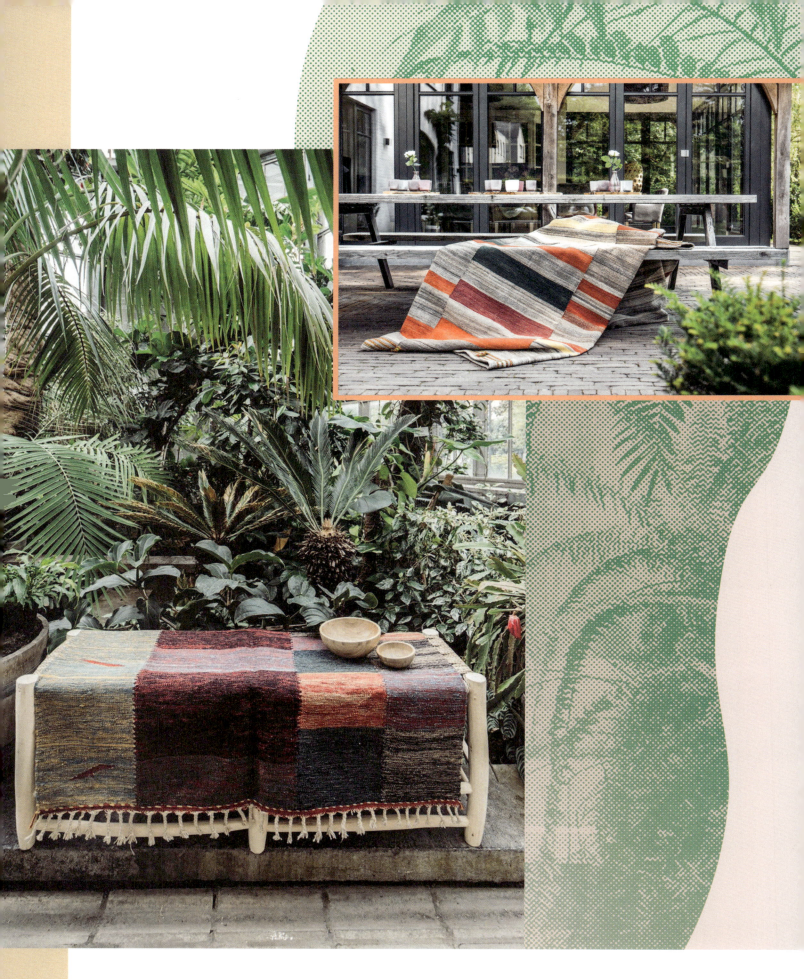

Outdoor

91

↗ The luxurious-looking *Mamounia Sky* rug, designed by Martyn Lawrence Bullard for British carpet house The Rug Company, bathes the outdoor space in an oriental atmosphere. The design is a modern update of a traditional Moroccan tile pattern.

← This majestic, monumental space begs for an exclusive carpet with generous dimensions, such as this hand-knotted carpet from the Kasmhir Blazed Collection by Belgian designer Thibault Van Renne.

→ If your garden is not in bloom for a while, the handwoven *Oaxaca* carpet offers solace. This design by Spanish carpet label Nanimarquina combines a geometric block pattern with colourful blossoms.

↑ The weathered peeling walls of abandoned buildings have a tactile effect. They were the inspiration for the Grunge carpet collection by Belgian designer Thibault Van Renne.

# How to

... choose the right colour
for your outdoor carpet
*De gustibus et coloribus non est disputandum*
'There is no accounting for tastes', goes the Latin
maxim. That said, in general we can say that light
colours make a patio look bigger and dark colours make
a space feel cosier and more intimate. Soft, subdued
shades go well with the surrounding nature, with a
modern garden with light furniture or in a Scandinavian
setting. Rust and brown tones work well with teak
furniture.

... choose the right place
for your outdoor carpet
In the garden, there is nothing like a relaxing
view of the surrounding greenery. A heavily furnished
living room with a generous view of an equally intensely
furnished terrace does not provide the ultimate zen
feeling. For this reason, avoid placing the rug and the
garden furniture set in the centre of the terrace; instead
set them off to the side, out of sight. In less obvious
places, such as next to the swimming pool or in an
unexpected spot in the garden, the rug becomes a real
eye-catcher.

... arrange furniture on an outdoor carpet
A common rule in larger outdoor spaces is to
place the front legs of the furniture on the rug. In this
way, the rug connects all the furniture and individual
elements with each other. Together, they form an island
that radiates calm and unity.

# Hilde Francq
# Francq Colors

Hilde Francq, the *eminence blonde* of Belgian trend watchers, knows like no other how to detect colours, materials, textures, patterns and shapes for your interior. For this she travels around the world, together with her team from trend studio Francq Colors – from London and Copenhagen, via Berlin and Milan, to New York and Tokyo. Her mission is anything but guesswork, because Francq states that a lot of interior trends find their origin in sociological phenomena. The COVID crisis, the anxieties of Generation Z and the advance of digitisation have not gone unnoticed in interior design circles. As an archaeologist of the future, Francq predicted, among other things, the revival of tactile and colourful carpets, long before they came on the scene. In the interview here, Francq also explains why tactiles and colours are becoming ever more important.

# 'The more digital our world becomes, the more we will appreciate the soft touch of a carpet.'

WWW.FRANCQCOLORS.BE

**What are the trends that we can expect in the coming years in the world of carpets?**

As we indicated in our most recent trend report, the theme of 'satisfaction' will become a very important trend. By this we mean that touches and experiences in the home should feel very satisfying. Carpets play a crucial role in this. In order to optimise the tactile aspect of carpets, we will see more and more high-pile carpets in the future; one might even call them 'wilderness carpets'. In one and the same carpet, you will also see an increasing variety of different pile heights, which will create the effect of a relief. We also notice that carpets are increasingly used to bring colour into the home. Colourful interiors are a huge trend, and carpets are a handy tool for this.

**Does the carpet have a future? And if so, which carpet categories in particular?**

Of course carpets have a future. The more digital our world becomes, the more we will appreciate the soft touch of a carpet. This is something that computers and apps can never match. In my opinion, the most important carpet categories are ecological carpets, allergy-free carpets and carpets that find themselves in the area between art and design. More and more, carpets are created by artists, which makes them ideal vehicles to combine art and design. It follows that wall-to-wall carpets will also remain popular. We are even seeing a comeback of the fitted carpet. With the revival of the seventies, suddenly everyone wants a seating area in their home, and of course this includes wall-to-wall carpet.

**How important are tactility and texture?**

Crucial. We have noticed since the COVID crisis how alienating it feels to have to avoid touch. In the coming years, we will compensate for this by bringing in as many tactile textures as possible.

**Does the colour of a carpet have an effect on the room?**

It is mainly the combination of floor and carpet that has an important effect on a room. *Ton-sur-ton* – that is, a carpet in almost the same colour as the floor – creates warmth and cosiness in a subtle way. If, on the other hand, the colour of the carpet is completely different from that of the floor, the carpet mainly has decorative value. Between these two extremes is an important grey area where you can play with different atmospheres.

**What do you need to consider when combining carpets with furniture, decorative items or art?**

It is mainly a question of choosing your accents in the house well. A striking carpet, a large work of art or a piece of furniture as an eye-catcher can quickly become too much. It is better to opt for one eye-catcher and choose the other pieces around it on the basis of that. Let colours and materials recur, and make sure that you do not cover a beautiful carpet with too many things. After all, there is no need to put anything on a carpet. If you have enough space, you can let the carpet attract all the attention.

**Has the carpet been moved to other rooms over the years?**

In the 1960s a carpet was traditionally placed under the dining table. Today the carpet has become free. It can be laid anywhere – in the bedroom, the bathroom, the hall or the kitchen. But the living room remains the most popular room for the decorative carpet. In the evening, you want to be able to stroke your bare feet over the carpet there. A real feeling of home.

**Do you have an 'all-time favourite' carpet?**

I am a big fan of the 'Feathers' collection by Maarten De Ceulaer at cc-tapis. A little tighter, but also very beautiful in almost any interior, is *Villa Tapis* by Axelle Vertommen, inspired by the interior of Villa Cavrois.

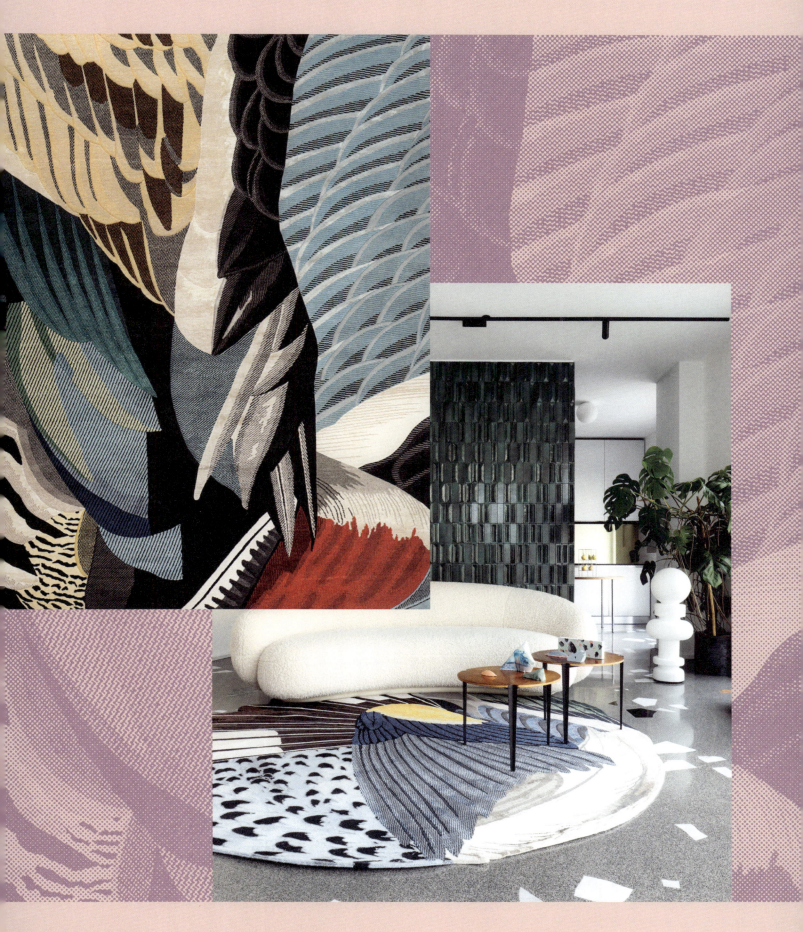

Interview

# Patterns

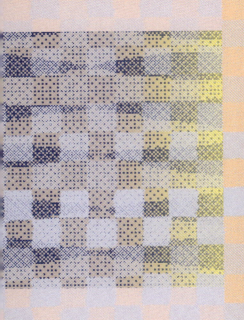

The patterned carpet is experiencing an unprecedented revival. This should not come as a surprise. History teaches us that patterns are exquisite vehicles for celebrating individuality and self-expression. Patterns are an inexhaustible source of delight among artists, architects and fashion designers.

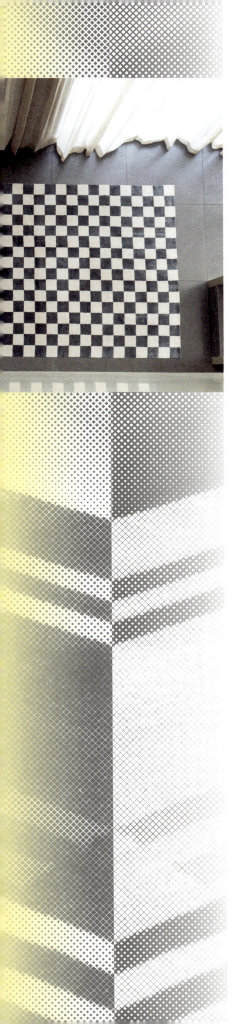

What would Louis Vuitton be without its famous checkerboard pattern? The checkerboard pattern of competitor Burberry, the Burberry check, is even protected as a registered trademark.

Brigitte Bardot aspired to the annals of history with her iconic wedding dress in bright-pink Vichy check. And Scottish tartan is likely to stay in your memory thanks to William Lawson's infamous commercial 'No Rules, Great Scotch', in which an entire Scottish clan shows off their crown jewels. The art world, too, recognises the power of recurring patterns. The Italian commedia dell'arte seems to have a patent on the harlequin diamond. And Dutch artist Piet Mondrian would probably be unknown were it not for his fiercely popular compositions of lines and colour planes.

No wonder all these iconic motifs are eagerly used in carpet country. In contemporary interiors, modern patterns are a hit. They are often based on the principle of repeating a single shape. Dots, stripes, bricks, diamonds, triangles and other geometric forms all work well in repetitive patterns. After all, repeating shapes, colours and materials usually bring calm and unity to the home. But abstract geometric prints from the modernist Bauhaus movement, for example, are also in full swing. Furthermore, quite a few patterned carpets play with optical illusions, in which our eyes play tricks on us. Vibrating colour fields and moiré patterns – in which two or more patterns are placed on top of each other at an oblique angle – guarantee compositions that suggest movement, or, even better, that seem to dance before our eyes.

Patterned carpets have a significant influence on how we perceive our interiors. For example, a long, narrow carpet with a vertical stripe pattern has an optical elongating effect, while horizontal lines optically widen the space. There are even carpets that gain depth through the use of both high-pile and low-pile yarns and enhance the strength of the pattern.

We are not part of the pattern police at all, but there are some golden rules to get the most out of your patterned carpet. Let the unbridled possibilities of the patterned carpets featured on the following pages provide you with rich inspiration. After all, patterns are for all times, all stripes and all tastes.

↙ Who dares to step on the *Hole* carpet, a trompe-l'œil design by Belgian designer Alain Gilles for RUGS by Yo² Design Studio. This collection plays with perception and creates the illusion of a gateway to somewhere else.

Patterns

Patterns

→ The luxurious *Piazzo* rug by Swiss carpet house Fischbacher brings the mystique of the East into your home. The carpet, which is made of merino wool and silk, is inspired by traditional tile mosaics from the Orient.

↓ It's as if the red carpet is being rolled out for you! An artful geometric design characterises this hand-knotted carpet from the Galanga collection by Mexican textile artist José Maria Balmaceda.

Carpets & Rugs

Carpets & Rugs

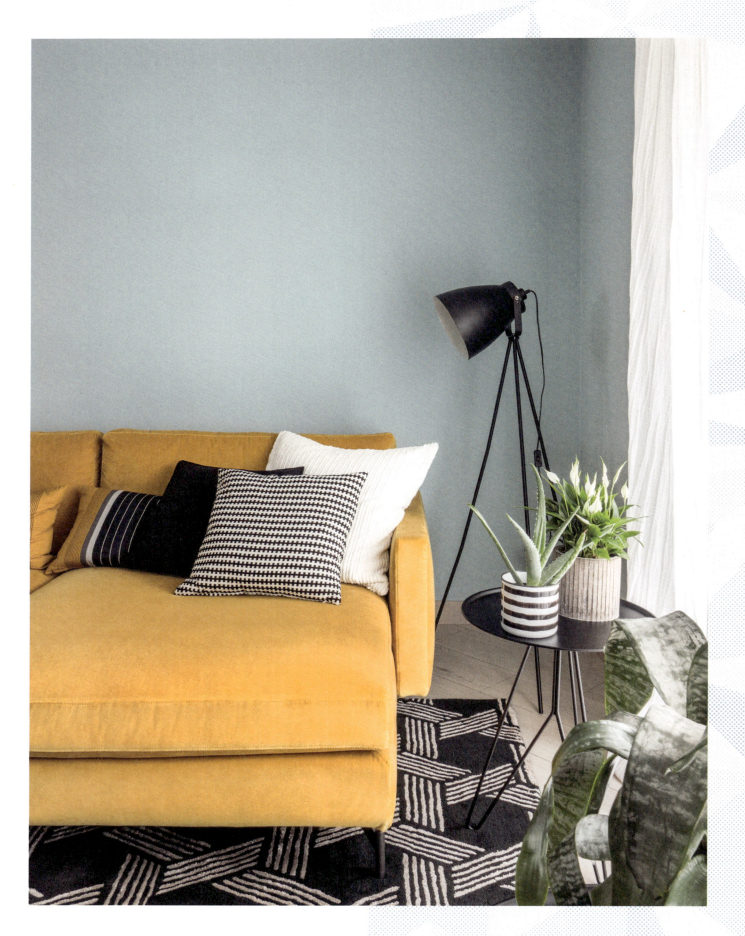

# How to

### ... combine different patterns

It seems a bit off-putting, but if you've set your sights on a bold interior and don't want to limit yourself to a single pattern, it's best to go for very different ones. The less the patterns look alike, the better. Otherwise, your brain will not notice the difference, and the whole thing will seem chaotic. In addition, different patterns give the room a playful character.

### ... optically lengthen or widen a space

A long, narrow carpet with a vertical striped pattern has an optically elongating effect, which is further enhanced by choosing fine vertical lines such as pinstripes. Conversely, wide, horizontal lines optically widen the space.

### ... combine bold colours and patterns

Repeat the colours of the patterned carpet throughout your interior – for example, in floors, walls, wallpaper, furniture, cushions, decorative items and even works of art. This creates coherence, depth and harmony, even if you sprinkle patterns and colours liberally.

# Shapes and sizes

For centuries, the quintessential shape of a rug has been rectangular, and it is unlikely that this will change anytime soon. However, there are some serious challengers on the prowl.

A rapid surge of sophisticated new design technologies has enabled designers to come up with exciting new shapes, including all sorts of organic forms, but also geometric figures and abstract, irregular shapes with jagged edges, cutouts and crazy angles.

These new shapes and sizes are great for children's rooms (think paw-print carpets, flowers, leaves, animals...) but can also be a real personality boost for the other spaces in your house. The only thing you need is the confidence to unleash your imagination!

The shape of a rug influences the style of a room, so it makes sense to contemplate which style you want to project. If you have traditional furnishings or are aiming for a traditional look in a room full of mixed-style furniture, a rectangular carpet will be your best choice. The same goes for square rugs, which also tend to be traditional.

Round rugs, on the contrary, will give a room an instant modern feel. Put a generously sized round rug under a round dining table, or scatter small round rugs around the room to anchor side tables and other small pieces of furniture. Round and oval rugs also go well with the organic shapes of seventies furniture and will give a room a warm, feminine feel, especially when they are made of cosy, shaggy materials.

There is good news for those who want to make a truly eye-catching statement with their choice of carpet, instead of merely adding an accent to a space. In the last couple years, renowned international designers like the Spanish Patricia Urquiola, the British Faye Toogood and the Brazilian Campana brothers have tried their hand at creating the craziest rug shapes for top brands like GAN, Nodus and cc-tapis. The results are stunning pieces of art you will want to show off in their full glory, instead of putting them under a table or sofa. They will become the focus of attention in your room.

Notably, these rugs are also completely customizable: you can choose the colour, pattern, material and size. As for materials, the choices are more elaborate than with traditional carpets. Apart from wool and silk, you will also find fabrics like felt and even recycled materials like PET. Carpets like these often come with eye-watering prices but are the antiques of the future, so are worth the investment.

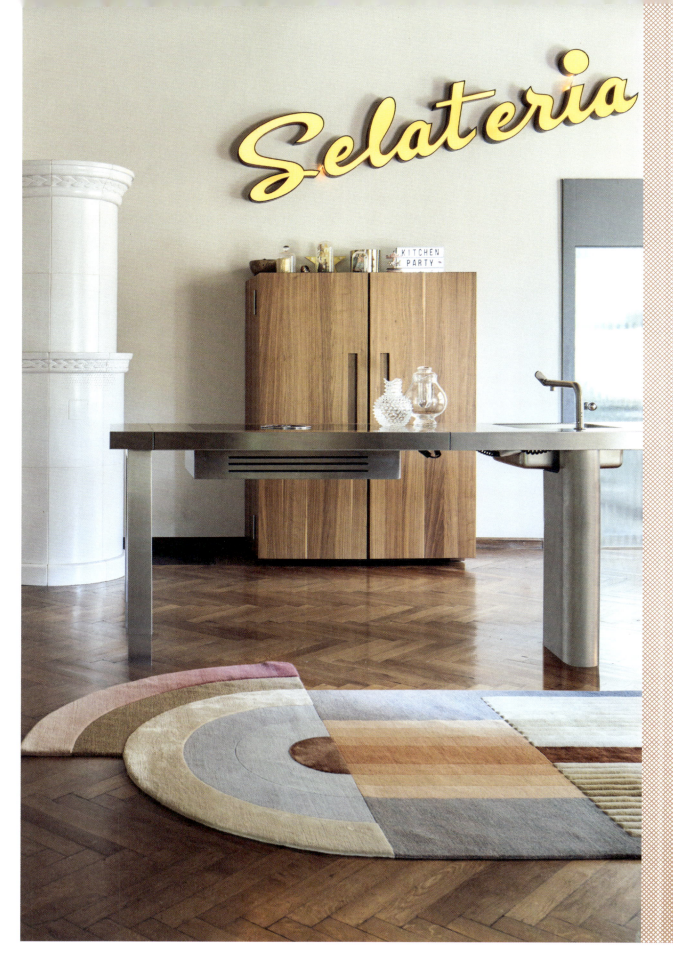

Interieurontwerp en styling:
Monique van der Reijden

→ Carpet Slinkie is a design by Patricia Urquiola for cc-tapis, hand-knotted in Nepal and a study of colours and shades, translated into organic shapes. Placed in full sight, it adds a joyous, fun accent to a room.

← A sculptural carpet adds a note of sophistication to this room. *Bliss Ultimate* is designed by Mae Engelgeer for cc-tapis and should really be called a 'textile landscape' instead of a carpet. It is a complex play of shapes, shades, materials and pile heights.

Carpets & Rugs

# How to

### ... know whether your carpet is the right size

If you have found the carpet of your dreams but you are not sure whether it is the right size, you can lay newspapers on the spot where the carpet will be placed. This will give you a visual impression of how big the carpet needs to be.

### ... determine the right shape for your carpet

The shape of your furniture will be a decisive factor. A sofa with rounded corners or a curved shape will go well with a softly shaped rug. If your furnishings are dominated by straight lines, then you could choose a geometric shape or jagged edges for your carpet.

### ... make your eye-catcher shine

The best place for your bold personal statement is in the centre of the room, as the main decoration. Combine it with white walls and curtains to make it the absolute focus of attention.

# Fien Muller and Hannes Van Severen
# Muller Van Severen

In 2011, Fien Muller and Hannes Van Severen, together the designer duo Muller Van Severen, made a blazing entrance into the design world with their first exhibition at valerie_traan gallery in Antwerp. Since the beginning of their collaboration, they have built an international career with increasing success. Since both designers are artists, it is not surprising that their designs balance on the seesaw between art and design. Colour, tactility and texture are the common denominators of their work, whether it concerns furniture or a rug. Internationally renowned carpet houses like Ashtari and cc-tapis also came knocking on their door and liked what they saw.

'Our love of materials is the starting point for many of our designs.'

Your love of materials is legendary, and the starting point of many of your designs. How important are tactility and texture for you?

Very important, because tactility also has to do with the attraction one experiences to want to touch something. Of course, touching is even more important when you design something like a rug, something that your body eventually comes into contact with, at least most of the time.

Besides your love of materials, colour is also your trademark. How do those colours come about? Do you have a certain colour philosophy?

Colour forms the character, the presence, the atmosphere of a work. We can hardly help but use colour. It is stronger than ourselves. We do see colour more as a material and not as something you add at the end of the production process. Colour is present in the creation and conception of a design. So it's not that we 'colour' a design, because the application of colour always happens very instinctively.

Apart from being designers, you are also artists. You can see that in your carpets *Ombra* and *Carpet Blue/Green* and *Carpet Blue/Yellow*. How did these designs come about?

In designing *Ombra*, we were looking for a way out of the two-dimensional plane that a carpet usually is. We wanted to step out of the flatness, as it were. With this in mind, we started cutting and pasting paper. We took photos of the result and then started playing with light and shadow. The shadows in the pattern add a geometric dimension to the carpet and create a three-dimensional effect.

*Muller: Carpet Blue/Green* and *Carpet Blue/Yellow* are based on my work as a photographer, where I focus on contemporary still lifes. With the collected photos, we made a collage together. The ribbons, the illustrations on the carpet, are a remnant of that.

Who or what inspired you?

It is a cliché, but daily life is our greatest source of inspiration. Everything and nothing. It could be an aubergine from the shop or the colour of something in a swimming pool. By living together, we are constantly pointing things out to each other. We are each other's greatest source of inspiration.

What can a carpet do for a room?

A carpet is a very interesting and rewarding object, because it is a connecting element in the space that interacts with all the objects present. A carpet acts as a kind of glue in the room and creates warmth. Not only the colour, but also the pattern and structure of a carpet have an effect on the room. Everything always has an effect on everything. A carpet can be very intimate. It invites you to take off your shoes and walk on it barefoot. There is something very sensitive about that.

What do you need to consider when combining carpets with design or art?

In our opinion you should see a carpet as an object in its own right and choose a design that you feel comfortable with. Something you want to look at and touch every day. That is the most important thing. The rest will follow.

# Traditional & transitional

If such a thing as the 'archetypal carpet' exists, it is probably what is called the traditional carpet. It's the Persian rug we played on as a child visiting our grandparents, the carpets we saw in stately homes and castles, the carpets in the windows of carpet galleries. These rugs are inspired by Oriental, Persian or European patterns that date back centuries.

The designs are usually ornate and intricate, with floral elements, borders and central medallions in geometric shapes. The colours of these carpets will depend on the dyes that existed at the time they were created. For Persian rugs this means warm hues like maroon, brown, sage, blue, beige and green, while tribal rugs will feature mainly earthy colours.

By choosing a traditional carpet, you bring a piece of history into your home, as these carpets are made with techniques and designs that have been passed on for centuries. Their rather majestic looks make them an excellent choice for the furnishing of formal spaces in homes or offices, where they will serve as the eye-catcher of the room.

A traditional rug is considered antique when it is 100 years old or more; vintage when it sits in the age range of 20–50 years old. New pieces can still be hand-knotted, but beware: they can also be 'hand-tufted' or machine-made. If hand-tufted or machine-made, they will not be unique and are hence less valuable.

Rather confusing is the carpet style that looks traditional but which, in reality, is not. We call these transitional rugs, because they combine features of both traditional and contemporary rugs, which makes them timeless and adaptable to many trends. Designers will borrow elements of traditional designs and play with them, making new compositions, rescaling them, adding contemporary colour schemes … the possibilities are endless.

The new designs that emerge from these creative ventures are in many ways very different from their traditional sisters. The designs are more playful, which makes the rugs less formal and very popular among homeowners all over the world. The contemporary colours make them an easy match for all sorts of interior styles. In minimalist homes, they bring a touch of warmth and focus, while in more classic surroundings they will spruce up a drab colour palette and add to the cosiness.

Whether you choose a traditional or a transitional rug is primarily a matter of taste, but it is helpful to keep in mind that traditional rugs are best suited for large spaces and less suitable for bedrooms or studies, as their designs will tend to break the quiet atmosphere you may be looking for.

↑ A precious Chinese Art Deco rug from Antique Oriental Rugs softens the straight, contemporary lines of this bathroom, with its vanity stand by Italian design brand Poliform and its taps by Dornbracht.

→ This gracefully detailed room is given even more elegance by adding a carpet from the French Savonnerie Collection by Thibault Van Renne. The colours of the carpet and the meticulously detailed design make it the focus of the space.

Thibault Van Renne

↑ A sunny room facing the garden is the perfect spot for a vintage rug, its colours reflecting the green of the garden. The fresh plants make the space feel like it is spring all year round.

→ In this interior by Parisian designer Véronique Cotrel, the contemporary design of the table and chairs effortlessly blends with an antique cabinet and a cheerfully coloured transitional carpet. The carpet combines a classic pattern with fashionable hues.

↑ This transitional carpet is part of the Kashmir Blazed collection by Belgian designer Thibault Van Renne. It is made of cashmere wool and bamboo silk, which revives the classic pattern and makes this living room come alive.

# How to

...    choose the material of your rug

If you are looking for a rug for an area with medium or low traffic, your best choice is wool or wool-silk. Pure silk is too delicate. If you really want your carpet to feature in a busy space, you could hang it on the wall.

...    tell the difference between a handmade rug and a machine-made rug

We can provide you with some rules of thumb. In a handmade rug, the fringe should be a part of the foundation; you will see on the back that it goes all the way through to the other side. Also, the edges will be less straight and may curl a little bit. Machine-made rugs have straight edges and very clean stitches, and the back will look very symmetrical.

...    take extra care of your rug

If you are worried about your traditional rug being worn down by your family life and losing some of its lustre, you can place a rug pad underneath. Not only will it preserve the pile of your rug by adding support, but it will also prevent slipping and will protect your floor.

# Floral

It is a sad truth that floral and botanical rugs are still too often thought of only as the favourite floor covering of old ladies in cosy cottages. Hence, many people decide that this theme is not suitable for the airy, modern living spaces of today. They couldn't be more wrong.

Floral and botanical rugs come in an endless variety – from delicately feminine to bold and graphic, from cutting-edge contemporary to timelessly traditional.

Let's start with the most light-hearted collections of summery carpets that bring a warm, exotic feel to your home. The simplest pieces are made of jute, hemp or cotton and give your room a relaxing holiday vibe, particularly if you combine them with simple whitewood or wicker furniture and accessories in natural colours. If the atmosphere that you are looking for is more that of a quirky, chic boutique hotel, you can opt for tropical prints of flowers, leaves or even animals. In doing so, you are inviting nature into your home, along with all the free and magical creatures that live there. Combined with rich colours, luxurious materials like velvet and silk and even a touch of gold, you can really walk on the wild side.

If the above ideas are too capricious for you, you can delve into the world of abstract, arty rugs, where you will also find floral and botanical themes, often with large flowers or leaves, in the most striking colours. If your house is light and modern, and decorated mainly in understated hues, a vibrant carpet can become the centrepiece of the room and add a touch of personality.

Last but not least, you find a lot of botanical themes in the collections of traditional and transitional rugs. Traditional floral rugs carry within them the rich and varied histories of regions and peoples all over the world, from the Caucasus to India. They are an amalgam of styles and handicrafts developed over the centuries. Transitional rugs are inspired by these carpets and mix their symbols with contemporary elements. Combine them with vintage fifties and sixties furniture for a retro look, a chesterfield seat and a well-filled bookcase for that English club feeling or a robust wooden sofa and sideboard if you prefer the simple life.

Finally, if you are looking for a surprise effect, experimenting with form might be the way to go. Why stick to the traditional rectangular form when today's technology allows the craziest shapes to be created? With the botanical theme, the inspirations are endless: animal shapes, leaves, flower buds, branches ... take your pick and amaze your guests!

↓ Bring the garden into your home with the leaf-shaped rug *Hydrangea* by Kiki Van Eijk for Nodus, paired with organically shaped furniture and, last but not least, a huge jug of flowers!

The *Flora* carpet by Barcelona artist Santi Moix for Nanimarquina is presented here in the stunning surroundings of the Casa Batlló Barcelona, designed by Antoni Gaudí. In this carpet, the artist explores the parallelism between life and death through his biomorphic flowers.

↓ The interiors of French designer Frédérique Trou-Roy are whimsical and wild, yet feminine and delicate. Here, Trou-Roy boldly mixes big and small floral patterns. Thanks to the slim-profiled furniture, white ceiling and simple stone floor, she gets away with it.

Floral

↗ *Feathers* is a carpet designed by Maarten De Ceulaer for cc-tapis, made entirely by hand in Himalayan wool and silk. To create each design, De Ceulaer used digitally processed and scanned photographs of bird species, playing with the resulting images and translating them into marvellous rugs.

This magnificent carpet is called *Painted Lady* and is a design by Alexander McQueen for The Rug Company. It depicts a butterfly in full flight and is made of wool and silk. The silk adds lustre and life to the warm colours of the rug, as if the rug is about to take off any minute.

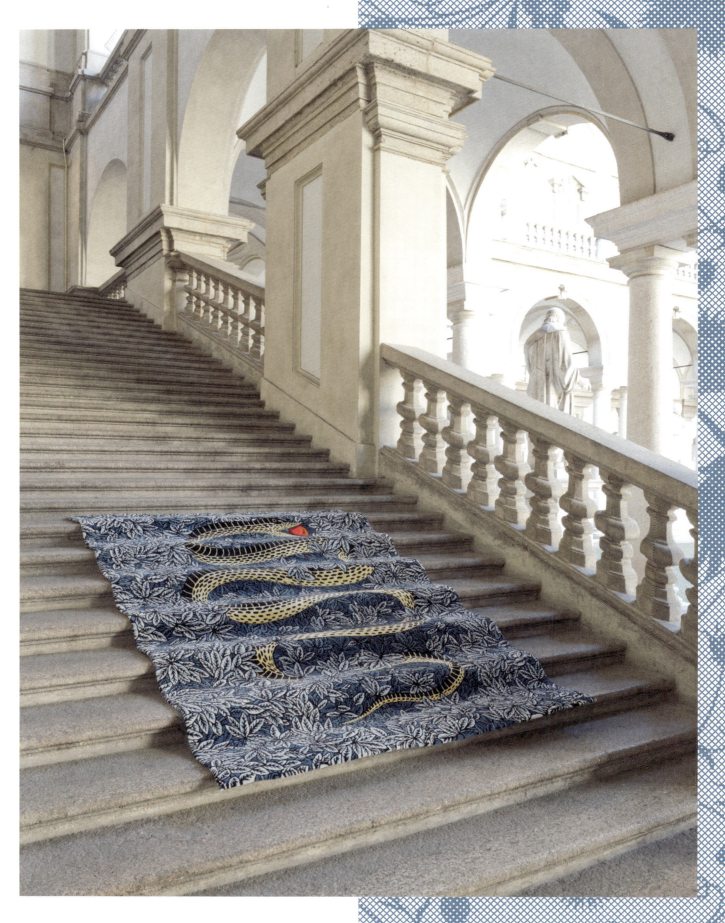

# How to

...    choose the right type of floral carpet for your space

This means skirting around some pitfalls. The right colour will depend on the atmosphere you want to create. Soft colours will create a cosy feeling, bright colours bring energy and personality, while black and white will guarantee a timeless and classy touch.

...    avoid visual chaos

It is important to pick the right primary (background) colour of the carpet, which in turn depends on the primary colour that is present in the other components of the room. If possible, choose your rug first, and use it to determine the rest of the furniture around it.

...    combine a floral rug with other patterns

You can mix flowers with dots, stripes and geometric designs, as long as you stick to these basic rules: keep other patterns smaller than the pattern of your rug, and choose only one hue which is also present in your rug. To avoid overkill, keep your curtains white or neutral.

# Christopher Mould
# Bazaar Velvet

Bazaar Velvet is a London rug company with over 30 years' experience, specialising in luxury designer rugs. They offer an elaborate selection of quality contemporary rugs, in a wide range of sizes. Many of those are creations of the in-house design team. They also have a bespoke design service at the disposal of customers who want a carpet customised to their own taste and space, changing colours, scale, size, shape and materials to meet their specifications. All rugs are hand-knotted and made of hand-spun high-quality wool or silk. Lovers of antique, vintage and classic rugs will also love the hand-picked, unique pieces from around the world the shop has at hand.

'Our rugs are not only sustainable, they are timelessly beautiful and unique. No two pieces are the same. In fact, you could say that they are pieces of art.'

### What sort of carpets does Bazaar Velvet specialise in?

We specialise in hand-knotted carpets: classic, antique, vintage and contemporary. The majority are our own design: we create paintings and send them to the loom, where they are transformed into rugs. Our paintings are often inspired by classical designs. We blow them up to a different scale, erase certain areas ... the result is familiar yet completely new. We have two in-house designers who work on this.

### Do you have special criteria for selecting rugs for your collections?

Criteria as such, no. We get random inspirations that set us off on an adventure. Or we look at history, nature ... some things will be more colourful, some things more restful. Anything can start it off, really, and it results in many different looks and styles.

### Are there trends in carpet design?

There certainly are. These last three or four years, Berber rugs were the big thing. Originally, they came from the Moroccan Atlas Mountains; now they are made everywhere, which has meant the end of this trend. Today, we see that colours are coming back. It seems people are getting bored with neutral hues and want to inject colour into their furnishings again.

We also have timeless pieces in our collection, like our Levantine gold rug. The inspiration was a photo of a rock formation in North Africa. It is organic and has lots of depth, and it's very luxurious with its gold silk and is easy to place. This piece will last generations.

### Has globalisation boosted carpet design or made it more uniform?

It has definitely boosted design. The world is a smaller place now. Designers try their hands at different products: ceramics, rugs, furniture ... Globalisation has created a lot more products and choice than there were 10 years ago. The surge in new technologies has helped, too. Today, once you have trusted manufacturers, you don't have to travel that much anymore.

### How has your business evolved over these last couple of years?

Very well! People seem to have rediscovered their homes, due to the COVID pandemic and the lockdown. Although we had to close the showroom for a couple of months, business went well. People were at home, they weren't travelling and hence decided to make their homes more appealing to live in. Many existing customers placed orders, and we made several new customers as well.

### How important is ecology for you?

When you work in a business such as ours, ecology goes without saying. Our carpets are handmade, and we work with only natural materials. We hardly use any technologies. So where sustainability is concerned, our products will last for generations. You really can't compare them to machine-made, synthetic rugs that will last only 10 years or so and will then be thrown away. Moreover, our rugs are not only sustainable, they are timelessly beautiful and unique. No two pieces are the same. In fact, you could say that they are pieces of art.

### That already is an answer to our last question: Do you consider your pieces art or design?

People look at them as functional pieces, but there is so much skilled work and so many precious materials involved, that we definitely consider them pieces of art.

# Credits

COVER 'Beetle' by Alexander McQueen for The Rug Company

P.12 'Sky Owls and the Puddels' from the collection 'Ava's Paintings' by Rive Roshan, produced by Moooi Carpets, distributed by Form Editions *Photography by Design & Practice*

P.14 'Wild' from the collection 'Magic Marker Carpets' by Moooi Carpets

P.16 Silhouette Collection by Jaime Hayon for Nanimarquina *Photography Albert Font*

P.17 Wall textile by Vera Roggli (design studio Wiesi Will), Black Ztista coffee table by Faina, Rocking Chair in off-white cotton by Tucurinca. WWW.OMARCITY.WORLD *Photography by Kaatje Verschoren*

P.18 'Hole Rugs' by Alain Gilles for Yo² Rugs, Traffic chair for Magis by Konstantin Grcic, Geoffrey mirror for Ligne Roset by Alain Gilles. WWW.ALAINGILLES.COM

P.19 'Apparence' by Xavier Lust for Nodus *Photography by Nicolas Schimp*

P.20 'Framis' by Mary Katrantzou for The Rug Company

P.21 *Photography by Montse Garriga Grau / Photofoyer*

P.22 *Photography by Montse Garriga Grau / Photofoyer*

P.24 *Photograpy by Montse Garriga Grau / Photofoyer*

P.25 *Photography by Rei Moon / Living Inside*

P.26 Sepulveda Arquitectos Time Capsules Collection for Balmaceda Studio *Photography by José Margaleff*

P.27 Design Studio Klass for cc-tapis, production & Styling by Alice Ida *Photography by Valentina Sommariva / Living Inside*

P.28 'Eclipse' by Kelly Behun for The Rug Company

P.30 'Brink Ivory' by Kelly Wearstler for The Rug Company

P.34 left *Photography by Manolo Yllera / Photofoyer*

P.34 right 'Deep pile Merino Axel' by The Rug Company

P.36 Carpet by Carine Boxy, Interior by Geraldine Vanheuverswijn *Photography by Stefanie Faveere*

P.37 Carpet by Carine Boxy, Interior by Caroline Notté *Photography by Jan Verlinde*

P.38 Saara Loop Concrete rug by Phenicia Concept *Photopgraphy by Montse Garriga Grau / Photofoyer*

P.40 top 'Pure' by Made Studio for GAN Rugs

P.40 bottom Carpet by Jacaranda Carpets & Rugs, sofa and cushions by Mark Alexander

P.41 'Pure' by Made Studio for GAN Rugs

P.42 Wellbeing Collection by Ilse Crawford for Nanimarquina *Photography by Salva Lopez*

P.44 left Design by Pascale Risbourg *Photography by Kaatje Verschoren*

P.44 right Kilim collection by Ethnicraft & Ashtari Carpets WWW.ASHTARICARPETS.COM *Photography by Nicolas Schimp*

P.45 Teotihuacan Collection by Balmaceda Studio *Photography by José Margaleff*

P.46 Romano Arquitectos *Photography by Manolo Yllera / Photofoyer*

P.48 Eleven Mechelen, WWW.ELEVENMECHELEN.BE *Photography by Kaatje Verschoren*

P.49 'Cootham' by Tjitske Storm for Revised *Photography by Studio Aksento*

P.50 *Photography by Alendra Meurant / Photofoyer*

P.51 Nomad collection by Ashtari Carpets WWW.ASHTARICARPETS.COM, *Photography by Claude Smekens voor Landelijk Wonen*

P.52 'Tres Vegetal' by Nani Marquina and Elise Padrón

*Photography by Albert Font*

P.53 design by Huis MORTIER *Photography by Kaatje Verschoren*

P.54 WWW.OMARCITY.WORLD *Photography by Kaatje Verschoren*

P.56 *Photography by The Cosmopolitan Chicken*

P.59 Courtesy of Koen van Mechelen WWW.LABIOMISTA.BE

P.62 'ZOE Kubb' by Daria Zinovatnaya for GAN Rugs

P.64 'After Matisse Rug' by Sonya Winner Studio

P.65 Rug by Morag Myerscough *Photography by Bénédicte Ausset Drummond / Photofoyer*

P.66 *Photography by Helenio Barbetta / Living Inside*

P.68 'ZOE Sool' by Daria Zinovatnaya for GAN Rugs

P.70 Interior by Koen Verkeyn en Chris Snik, WWW.CHRISSNIK.COM *Photography by Kaatje Verschoren*

P.71 Carpet by Stark Carpet NY *Photography by Bénédicte Ausset Drummond / Photofoyer*

P.72 'Ruffle Sage' by Martin Brudnizki for The Rug Company

P.74 'Vintage Monumental Carpet' by Michel Boyer for Paraphe *Photography by Julie Ansiau / Photofoyer*

P.75 Artline Collection by Thibault Van Renne

P.76 'Moss Green Squiggle Rug' by Okej Studio

P.77 'Pink Squiggle Rug' by Okej Studio

P.78 Painting by Albert Pepermans *Photography by Kaatje Verschoren*

P.79 'Pole position' by Klaartje Busselot for Kiiv *Photography by Kaatje Verschoren*

P.80 *Photography by Claudia Zalla / Photofoyer*

P.84 left Carpet by Ashtari Carpets WWW.ASHTARICARPETS.COM, styling by Jana Rymen *Photography by Evenbeeld*

P.85 right *Photography by Alexandra Meurant / Photofoyer*

P.86 Shade Outdoor Collection by Begüm Cana Özgür for Nanimarquina *Photography by Albert Font*

P.87 Shade Outdoor Collection by Nani Marquina and Elisa Padrón *Photography by Albert Font*

P.88 Layers Collection by Patricia Urquiola for GAN Rugs

P.90 left Carpet by Ashtari Carpets WWW.ASHTARICARPETS.COM, styling by Jana Rymen *Photography by Evenbeeld*

P.90 right Carpet Design Kilim by Ashtari Carpets WWW.ASHTARICARPETS.COM *Photography by Claude Smekens voor Landelijk Wonen.*

P.91 Carpet by Ashtari Carpets WWW.ASHTARICARPETS.COM, styling by Jana Rymen *Photography by Evenbeeld*

P.92 'Mamounia Sky' design by Martyn Lawrence Bullard for The Rug Company

P.94 Kashmir Blazed Collection by Thibault Van Renne

P.95 'Diamond' by Charlotte Lancelot for GAN Rugs

P.96 'Lamu Sun' by Nicole Fuller for The Rug Company

P.98 Design by Modullar Architects *Photography by Celestyna Krol / Photofoyer*

P.99 Oaxaca Outdoor Collection by Nani Marquina for Nanimarquina *Photography by Albert Font*

P.100 Carpet by Ashtari Carpets WWW.ASHTARICARPETS.COM *Photography by Claude Smekens voor Landelijk Wonen.*

P.101 Grunge Collection by Thibault Van Renne

P.102 *Photography by Montse Garriga Grau / Photofoyer*

P.104 Courtesy of Hilde Francq

P.107 left 'feathers' by Maarten de Ceulaer for cc-tapis

P.107 right 'feathers' by Maarten de Ceulaer for cc-tapis, Francesco Librizzi architect and designer and artistic director of Fontana Arte, Production: Francesca Sironi

*Photography by Monica Spezia / Living Inside*

P.110 left Kilim collection by Ethnicraft & Ashtari Carpets WWW.ASHTARICARPETS.COM *Photography by Nicolas Schimp*

P.110 right Balmaceda Studio *Photography by Fabián Martinez*

P.112 Roots collection by Inma Bermudez for GAN Rugs

P.114 'Tucurinquita' by Tucurinca, El Banco zapa, Aichuchi Bench by Tucurinca. WWW.OMARCITY.WORLD *Photography by Kaatje Verschoren*

P.116 'Hole Rugs' by Alain Gilles for Yo² Rugs

P.116 left 'Hole Rugs' by Alain Gilles for Yo² Rugs, Traffic chair for Magis by Konstantin Grcic, WWW.ALAINGILLES.COM

P.118 'Bravado Graphite' by Kelly Wearstler for The Rug Company

P.119 Christian Fischbacher

P.120 *Photography by Kaatje Verschoren*

P. 122 left Sepulveda Arquitectos Galanga Collection by Balmaceda Studio *Photography by José Margaleff*

P.122 right 'Piazzo' by Christian Fischbacher

P.123 Blur Collection by Ronan & Erwan Bouroullec for Nanimarquina *Photography by Albert Font*

P.124 Carpet by Ashtari Carpets WWW.ASHTARICARPETS.COM *Photography by Claude Smekens voor Landelijk Wonen*

P.125 Moooi Carpets

P.126 *Photography by Cristina Bohman Galliena / Photofoyer*

P.130 top 'Bubbles Rug' by Sonya Winner Studio

P.130 bottom 'Lace with a carpet face' by Nika Zupanc for Nodus, direction and production by Laura Pozzi

P.132 cc-tapis, Styling Francesca Davoli *Photography by Fabrizio Cicconi / Photofoyer*

P.133 'Tidal carpet' by Germans Ermičs for cc-tapis, Accordo

coffee table by Charlotte Perriand for Cassina, Project: Studio Concepta, Luigi Di Mauro Morandi (architect) and Alice Frana (designer), Styling: Chiara Dal Canto *Photography by Helenio Barbetta / Living Inside*

P.134 'Grypho Terra Incognita' by Faberhama for Nodus, direction and production by Laura Pozzi

P.135 'Phoenix Terra Incognita' by Faberhama for Nodus, direction and production by Laura Pozzi

P.136 Villa Empain *Photography by Kaatje Verschoren*

P.138 'Doodles' by Faye Toogood for cc-tapis, interior design and styling: Monique van der Reijden, @moniquevanderreijden *Photography by Kaatje Verschoren*

P.140 'Ouroboros Terra Incognita' by Faberhama for Nodus, direction and production by Laura Pozzi

P.141 'Slinkie' by Patricia Urquiola for cc-tapis, styling Francesca Davoli *Photography by Fabrizio Cicconi / Photofoyer*

P.142 *Photography by Rei Moon (Moon Ray Studio) / Living Inside*

P.144 'Invaders rugs' by cc-tapis, production Chiara dal Canto *Photography by Helenio Barbetta / Living Inside*

P.145 *Photography by Manolo Yllera / Photofoyer*

P.146 top Stylist Laura Mauceri *Photography by Cristina Bohman Galliena / Photofoyer*

P.146 bottom 'Utltimate Bliss' by Mae Engelgeer for cc-tapis, Styling Francesca Davoli *Photography by Fabrizio Cicconi / Photofoyer*

P.147 *Photography by Richard Powers*

P.148 'Double Slinkie' by Patricia Urquiola for cc-tapis *Photography by Helenio Barbetta / Living Inside*

P.150 'Speckled Squiggle Rug' by Okej Studio

P.152 'Ombra' by Muller Van Severen for cc-tapis

*Photography by Frederik Vercruysse*

P.155 top: 'Blue/yellow' by Muller Van Severen x Ashtari Carpets *Photography by Fien Muller*

P.155 bottom: 'Ombra' by Muller Van Severen for cc-tapis *Photography by Claudia Zalla*

P.158 left 'Kazak Space Shifter' by CCtapis *Photography by Monica Spezia / Living Inside*

P.158 right 'Perished Persian' by Studio Job for Nodus *Photography by Dennis Brandsma*

P.160 Art Deco Chinese rug by Antique Oriental Rugs *Photography by Richard Powers / Photofoyer*

P.161 French Savonnerie Collection by Thibault Van Renne

P.162 Kashmir Blazed Collection by Thibault Van Renne

P.164 *Photography by Rei Moon (Moon Ray Studio) / Living Inside*

P.165 top *Photography by Rei Moon (Moon Ray Studio) / Living Inside*

P.165 bottom *Photography by Ruth Maria Murphy / Living Inside*

P.166 *Photography by Mauricio Fuertes / Photofoyer*

P.167: 'Estambul' by Javier Mariscal for Nanimarquina *Photography by Albert Font*

P.168 Carpet by Ashtari Carpets WWW.ASHTARICARPETS.COM styling by Jana Rymen *Photography by Evenbeeld*

P.169 *Photography by Julie Ansiau / Photofoyer*

P.170 Design by Studio Ati Dubai *Photography by Chiara Cadeddu / Photofoyer*

P.171 *Photography by Montse Garriga Grau / Photofoyer*

P.172 *Photography by Alexandra Meurant / Photofoyer*

P.174 Kashmir Blazed Collection by Thibault Van Renne

P.175 Handmade carpet from Afghanistan, furniture by Wegner *Photography by Ragnar Hartvig / Photofoyer*

P.176 *Photography by Catherine Gailloud / Photofoyer*

P.180 'Flores Rug' from the AYTM Flores Collection, Design by AYTM and Signe Kejlbo

P.182 'Hydrangea' by Kiki Van Eijk for NODUS *Photography by Valentia Sommariva*

P.183 'Pop Palms Rug' by Ilaria Ferraro Toueg for Ted Design Collection, Stylist Cristina Nava *Photography by Valentina Sommariva / Living Inside*

P.184 'Tree Trunk Rug' by Sonya Winner Studio

P.185 'Floreo Rug' design by AYTM and Signe Kejlbo

P.186 'Flora Collection' by Santi Moix for Nanimarquina *Photography by Albert Font*

P.188 *Photography by Julie Ansiau / Photofoyer*

P.189 *Photography by Julie Ansiau / Photofoyer*

P.190 'Tropic' by Christian Fischbacher

P.191 'Aureola' by Christian Fischbacher

P.192 'feathers' by Maarten de Ceulaer for cc-tapis, Francesco Librizzi architect and designer and artistic director of Fontana Arte, Production: Francesca Sironi *Photography by Monica Spezia / Living Inside*

P.194 'Glasswings' by Alexander McQueen for The Rug Company

P.195 'Tree of Life' by Alexander McQueen for The Rug Company

P.196 'Painted Lady' by Alexander McQueen for The Rug Company

P.198 'Beetle' by Alexander McQueen for The Rug Company

P.199 *Photography by Richard Powers / Photofoyer*

P.200 *Photography Anna Positano and Gaia Cambiaggi, courtesy Fornasetti*

p202 Courtesy of Bazaar Velvet

WWW.LANNOO.COM
Sign up for our newsletter with news about
new and forthcoming publications on art,
interior design, food & travel, photography
and fashion as well as exclusive offers and
events. If you have any questions or comments
about the material in this book, please do not
hesitate to contact our editorial team:
ART@LANNOO.COM

TEXTS
Karolien Van Cauwelaert
Karin Van Opstal

EDITING
Amy Haagsma

BOOK DESIGN
Superset WEARESUPERSET.BE

©Lannoo Publishers, Belgium, 2022
D/2022/45/247 – NUR450/454
ISBN: 978-94-014-7692-8

WWW.LANNOO.COM

All the rights reserved. No part of this publication may
be reproduced or transmitted in any form or by any
means, electronic or mechanical, including photography,
recording or any other information storage and retrieval
system, without prior permission in writing from the
publisher.

Every effort has been made to trace copyright holders.
If however you feel that you have inadvertently been
overlooked, please contact the publishers.